BIT WARS

Cyber Crime, Hacking

& Information Warfare

Dr. Thomas S. Hyslip

Library of Congress Control Number: 2015910344

CreateSpace Independent Publishing Platform, North Charleston, SC

ISBN: 1514673150

ISBN-13: 978-1514673157

CONTENTS

ACKNOWLEDGMENTS

This book would not have been possible without the assistance of many people. I want to thank Gary for his help with the cover and recommended content. Tom for his encouragement and support. And of course my family, Susan and Reagan.

COVER ART

Jan Paolo Cruz

POW Graphix Unlimited

Janpaolocruzrn@yahoo.com

1

INTRODUCTION

On October 11, 2012, Secretary of Defense Leon Panetta warned of an impending "Cyber Pearl Harbor": a cyber-attack against critical infrastructure combined with a simultaneous physical attack [1]. The results would be catastrophic, inflicting both physical damage and loss of life. Panetta further explained that foreign actors -- state sponsored terrorists or criminals -- had already probed America's critical infrastructure, and many large corporations had been attacked with distributed denial of service attacks and sophisticated malicious software (malware) [1]. Surprisingly to most, these types of cyber-attacks are a daily occurrence. Criminals, terrorists, and nations use the internet to commit crimes, raise money, spread propaganda, and steal secrets.

Many people still believe that cyber warfare will not come to their doorstep. Why would a criminal or hacker target me? The answer is: they won't. Cyber criminals don't target *people* without cause. But they do target any computer with a vulnerability. So while you personally may not be a target, your computer, smart phone, or tablet is. More specifically, your computer or any computer that contains your personable identifiable information (PII), credit card, bank account information, or email address, is a target. Are you certain that every computer containing your information is secure without any vulnerabilities?

Honestly, you can never be 100% certain you are protected unless you give up modern day technologies such as computers, smart phones, and the internet. And who wants to do that? But, you can take steps to increase your protection. You have taken an important first step: reading this book to learn who, what, where, why, and how cyber criminals, hackers, terrorists and nations commit cybercrime.

This books provides a history of cybercrime, cyber-terrorism, information warfare, and cyber espionage, leading to the current state of affairs. It is intended to provide an overview of cybercrime and why everyone should be concerned.

Chapter References

[1] (Panetta, 2012)

2

HISTORY OF CYBER-CRIME AND HACKING

Pinpointing the first commission of a cyber-crime is quite difficult, but many refer to it as John Draper's use of the Cap'n Crunch whistle to make free telephone calls in 1971 [1]. Draper realized the whistle produced a 2600 Hz tone which was the frequency used by the AT&T telephone networks to enter operator mode, and this enabled Draper to make his calls free of charge [1]. Draper continued to experiment with the phone system and built *blue boxes* to hack the phone system to further this agenda [2]. The blue box connected to a telephone and emitted audio tones to hack the system. Draper then began to sell the blue boxes, and even showed Steve Wozniak and Steve Jobs how to build their own [2]. Draper was arrested three times between 1972 and 1978 for telephone fraud.

The hacker society, 2600, www.2600.com, is named after the 2600 Hz tone and publishes a quarterly journal that is popular with hackers. At the time Draper was experimenting with the Cap'n Crunch whistle (Figure 1), the term *phreakers* was used to describe people who explored and experimented with the phone systems. Phreaking was the act of hacking the phone system and making calls for free. Phreakers nowadays are considered hackers because phone systems use the same technology as the internet.

Figure 1. The famous Cap'n Crunch Whistle

Also in 1971, Bob Thomas of BBN Technologies wrote the first computer worm called The Creeper and launched it on the ARPANET [3]. The ARPANET was the first packet switched network, created in 1969, and the forefather of the internet. We will cover the ARPANET in detail later. The Creeper worm was a self-replicating program that searched for remote computers, copied itself to the computer it found, displayed the message, "I'm the creeper, catch me if you can!" and then continued it's vicious cycle with other systems [3]. It is important to remember at this time ARPANET was only connected to certain universities and military installations, and this was not considered a crime but rather a practical joke.

The first computer virus to spread outside a laboratory environment is reported to be the Elk Cloner virus written in 1982 by a 15 year old, Rick Skrenta [4]. The virus was spread through floppy disks (Figure 2) and affected Apple II computer system's boot sector. Skrenta was interviewed by John Leyden of The Register on December 14, 2012, in honor of the 30 year anniversary of the release of Elk Cloner. The interview provides a good insight into the thinking of hackers of the time.

Figure 2. Original Elk Cloner Floppy Disk (Source: www.the register.co.uk)

Skrenta recalled how friends would share computer programs on floppy disks, and he thought it would be funny to play a prank on his friends [4]. Skrenta decided to, "booby trap new games to put up a message" and after a few pranks no one wanted to trade floppy disks with him. So Skrenta decided to see if he could create a program to alter the data on a floppy disk without ever touching it [4]. The result was the Elk Cloner virus. The virus wasn't intended to do any damage, but instead a practical joke. Every fifth reboot of the computer, the Elk Cloner would display a poem:

"Elk Cloner: The program with a personality. It will get on all your disks It will infiltrate your chips Yes it's Cloner!

It will stick to you like glue It will modify ram too Send in the Cloner!" [4]

The first arrest of hackers for cybercrime in the USA was reported in the Detroit Free Press on August 28, 1983. The FBI arrested seven boys between the ages of 16 and 25, identifying as a group called the "414s", who hacked into over 60 computers including the Las Alamos National Laboratory [5]. Charges were eventually dropped against the 414s, but this was a serious wake up call to information technologies professionals, law enforcement and the government. The interesting part of the story, there was no federal crime for hacking at the time, so the teenagers were originally charged with trespassing.

The U.S. Government passed the first legislation that made computer hacking a federal crime shortly after the 414s were caught. The Comprehensive Crime Control Act of 1984 gave the US Secret Service authority over Credit Card Fraud and Computer Fraud. The two U.S. laws resulting from the Act were 18 United States Code, Sections 1029 and 1030. The laws cover credit card fraud and computer fraud respectively. It is very ironic that these two laws were passed together. At the time of the Act, cybercrime was not an active part of credit card fraud. However, the two crimes are now intertwined and often one is committed as an underlying act of the other. In 1986, Congress amended 18 USC, Section 1030 with the Computer Fraud and Abuse Act. Since 1986, 18 USC Section 1030 has been amended eight times to address the increased sophistication of cyber crimes.

In 1988 the CERT Coordination Center (CERT-CC) was formed at the Software Engineering Institute, Carnegie Mellon University. The CERT-CC's mission is to provide timely and relevant cybersecurity research and solutions to cybersecurity challenges (CERT-CC, 2014). The same agency that funded the development of the ARPANET, the Advanced Research Projects Agency, also funded the establishment of the CERT-CC.

During the late 1980s and 1990s, there were numerous cyber-crimes, primarily viruses and worms, but also some notorious hackers. In 1988, the Morris Worm was released and affected almost one third of the internet at the time, resulting in the formation of the CERT-CC [1]. In 1991, the Michelangelo virus was released, and in 1999, the Melissa worm caused billions of dollars in damage by infecting

Microsoft Word documents and spreading through email messages. Many corporations were victims of denial of service attacks because the Melissa worm sent so many email messages. to (insert wherever/whoever it caused damage to, readers will connect more if they can visualize the exact effects) [1].

One of the most notorious cyber criminals in American history is Kevin Mitnick. Mitnick was first convicted of hacking into DEC's computer network in 1998, and was sentenced to one year in prison followed by 3 years of supervised release [6]. Towards the end of his supervised release, Mitnick hacked into Pacific Bell's computers and fled from justice [6].

Mitnick was a fugitive on the run for two and half years (Figure 3). During this time Mitnick hacked into numerous computers, stole passwords, and cloned cellular phones [6]. He also hacked into Tsutomu Shimomura's personal computer. Shimomura was a computer security and cellular phone expert who testified before Congress in 1992.

As a result of Mitnick's attack on Shimomura, Shimomura agreed to help the FBI track down Mitnick [6]. On February 15, 1995, Mitnick was arrested by the FBI in Raleigh, NC, ending the longest hacking fugitive case in history [6].

After the turn of the century, the rate of cybercrime continued to increase, as did access to the internet from home computers. As a result, the damages and losses caused by cybercrime grew exponentially. In 2001, the FBI / National White Collar Crime Center joint Internet Fraud Report showed a total of 16,755 complaints of cybercrime for a total loss of $17.8 million. By 2005, there were 231,493 complaints received and reported losses of over $183 million. In 2009, the complaints number over 336,000 and the reported losses topped $559 million. In the latest FBI report for 2013, the number of complaints topped 262,000 and reported losses was over $781 million. Yet, these statistics only reflect

Figure 3. A U.S. Marshals wanted poster for Kevin Mitnick

reported incidents and losses, and many cybercrime incidents go unreported. In 2014, McAfee estimated the total cost of cybercrime to be between $375 billion and $575 billion.

The recent attacks on Target and Home Depot highlight the growing threat of cybercrime. Both Target and Home Depot were affected by malware that captured the credit card information swiped at the register or point of sale (POS) terminal [7]. Combined, the two attacks stole over 90 million credit cards numbers [8].

Even more concerning than the number of stolen credit cards is that these attacks could have been prevented. The Target breach occurred because Target was using a home grown software running on a version of Windows XP, which was released in 2001 [9]. Furthermore, BlackPOS, the malicious software used to compromised the computers, was previously identified by Symantec and the FBI as known malware [9]. The Home Depot attack also occurred because of the company using an outdated Operating System (the same as seen with the Target breach) [10].

Almost any crime committed today can be carried out through a computer. In fact, many traditional crimes have been converted to cybercrimes. The remaining chapters will look at many of these crimes in detail, as well as cyber terrorism, information warfare, and cyber espionage.

Chapter References

[1] (Wrinkler, 2007)

[2] (Rhoads, 2007)

[3] (Chen & Robert, 2004)

[4] (Leyden, 2012)

[5] (Covert, 1983)

[6] (Christensen, 1999)

[7] (Lawrence & Riley, 2014)

[8] (Banjo, 2014; Wallace, 2013)

[9] (Smith, 2014)

[10] (Mick, 2014)

3

HACKERS AND CYBER CRIMINALS

The original hackers were not criminals, but simple *computer geeks* who tried to overcome the limitations of early computers. Often, the hackers' work lead to improvements and new computing designs. A good example of this was the start of Microsoft and their first software, Altair Basic. Since neither Bill Gates nor Paul Allen owned an Altair computer, they used an emulator written by Paul Allen on a Harvard University PDP-10 mainframe computer to write and test the Basic interpreter for the Altair [1]. At that time Harvard University, had no written policy for the use of the

PDP-10 mainframe computer. However, when Harvard learned that Allen and Gates were using the mainframe to emulate an Altair, the university would not allow Allen and Gates to finish their work. Gates and Allen were forced to purchase time on a private computer and went on to complete their work. In today's world, Gates and Allen would be forced to reimburse Harvard for the unauthorized use of the PDP-10 mainframe computer, or even worse face criminal charges for unauthorized use of the PDP-10.

Rather ironically, when computer hobbyists made copies of Microsoft's Altair Basic interpreter for friends, Gates accused the hobbyists of theft. This shows the attitude of hackers at the time. Open sharing of information and a quest for knowledge were hallmarks of individuals engaged in computer hacking and it was not seen as illegal to share software.

-2-

February 3, 1976

An Open Letter to Hobbyists

To me, the most critical thing in the hobby market right now is the lack of good software courses, books and software itself. Without good software and an owner who understands programming, a hobby computer is wasted. Will quality software be written for the hobby market?

Almost a year ago, Paul Allen and myself, expecting the hobby market to expand, hired Monte Davidoff and developed Altair BASIC. Though the initial work took only two months, the three of us have spent most of the last year documenting, improving and adding features to BASIC. Now we have 4K, 8K, EXTENDED, ROM and DISK BASIC. The value of the computer time we have used exceeds $40,000.

The feedback we have gotten from the hundreds of people who say they are using BASIC has all been positive. Two surprising things are apparent, however. 1) Most of these "users" never bought BASIC (less than 10% of all Altair owners have bought BASIC), and 2) The amount of royalties we have received from sales to hobbyists makes the time spent of Altair BASIC worth less than $2 an hour.

Why is this? As the majority of hobbyists must be aware, most of you steal your software. Hardware must be paid for, but software is something to share. Who cares if the people who worked on it get paid?

Is this fair? One thing you don't do by stealing software is get back at MITS for some problem you may have had. MITS doesn't make money selling software. The royalty paid to us, the manual, the tape and the overhead make it a break-even operation. One thing you do do is prevent good software from being written. Who can afford to do professional work for nothing? What hobbyist can put 3-man years into programming, finding all bugs, documenting his product and distribute for free? The fact is, no one besides us has invested a lot of money in hobby software. We have written 6800 BASIC, and are writing 8080 APL and 6800 APL, but there is very little incentive to make this software available to hobbyists. Most directly, the thing you do is theft.

What about the guys who re-sell Altair BASIC, aren't they making money on hobby software? Yes, but those who have been reported to us may lose in the end. They are the ones who give hobbyists a bad name, and should be kicked out of any club meeting they show up at.

I would appreciate letters from any one who wants to pay up, or has a suggestion or comment. Just write me at 1180 Alvarado SE, #114, Albuquerque, New Mexico, 87108. Nothing would please me more than being able to hire ten programmers and deluge the hobby market with good software.

Bill Gates

Bill Gates
General Partner, Micro-Soft

Figure 4. Bill Gates Letter (Source: Homebrew Computer Club Newsletter, January 1976)

However, as computers became more prevalent and interconnected, businesses and the government began to see hackers as a problem. The movie *War Games (1983)* is good illustration of the times. In the film, a young hacker is trying to connect to remote computers through war dialing a modem, and accidently connects to a military computer that controls nuclear weapons. In response to the growing problems, Congress passed the Comprehensive Crime Control Act of 1984.

In the 1980s, the terms "hacker" and "hacking" became synonymous with criminal activity. Hackers tried to distance themselves from these criminals by dubbing criminal activity with computers "cracking". Those who committed criminal acts were called "crackers". The term never caught on with the public or media, however. Still, the term is used on many IT related certification tests, including the Certified Information Systems Security Professional (CISSP) and the Certified Ethical Hacker (CEH) exams [2].

The access to home computers and high speed internet grew at a rapid pace at the turn of the century and so did daily use. The computer became more than a tool for business or school, it was now used for online banking, shopping, and sending friendly email messages. The increased use of credit cards and online banking spurred a new wave of criminals, cyber criminals.

Cyber criminals are not at all similar to the original hackers. Foremost, they are not motivated by curiosity or knowledge. Rather, they are pure criminals, looking to steal anything of value (e.g., financial data, such as credit card numbers and online banking credentials). Cyber criminals are also interested in personal identifiable information (PII), such as social security numbers and date of birth, which enables them to steal identities.

With the growth of cybercrime and the ability to commit cybercrime from anywhere in the world, numerous criminal organizations became involved. The Nigerian / West African criminal organizations took advantage of email to increase their ability to commit advance fee fraud[3]. Advance fee fraud is an email message or letter asking for assistance to transfer large sums of money from a foreign country to the United States. The letter is addressed from a fictitious government official and asks for financial assistance (an advance fee) to assist with the money transfer, in exchange for a percentage of the money transferred. In addition to the use of email to perpetrate the crime, the criminals also use computers and the internet to transfer the money from the victim.

Cyber criminals originally stole credit card information via physical means, rather than online, but used the internet to transfer the stolen credit card numbers overseas to make fraudulent purchases. Asian organized crime groups used a *skimmer* (Figure 5) device to capture credit card information at restaurants[4].

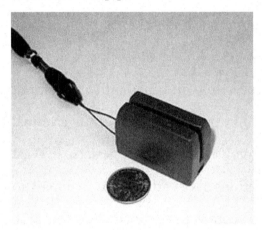

Figure 5. An example of a Credit Card Skimmer.

When a waiter takes a customer's credit card for payment, the waiter scans the credit card with the skimmer and the digital information is captured for future use. A small skimmer is capable of storing thousands of credit card's data and fits in a pocket.

While skimming at restaurants is still active, a new form of skimming has emerged. Cyber criminals now install skimmers on ATMs and steal the debit card information. The skimmers fit over the top of existing ATMs and do affect the use of the machine. Therefore, most ATM users are unaware their debit card information has been stolen. In addition to the skimmer, cyber criminals use a hidden camera and keypad overlay to steal the user's PIN (Figure 6).

While skimming is an active crime, the vast majority of cybercrime is now committed by Botnets and Malware. A Botnet is a network of compromised computers, which are controlled by an administrator or Botmaster, through common Internet communication protocols, including Internet Relay Chat (IRC), Peer-to-Peer (P2P), and Hypertext Transfer Protocol (HTTP)[5]. The computers that form the Botnet have been compromised with malicious software, and the Botmaster is able to capture and steal data directly from the computers. The majority of botnets automatically steal login names and passwords, credit card information, and *PII* data.

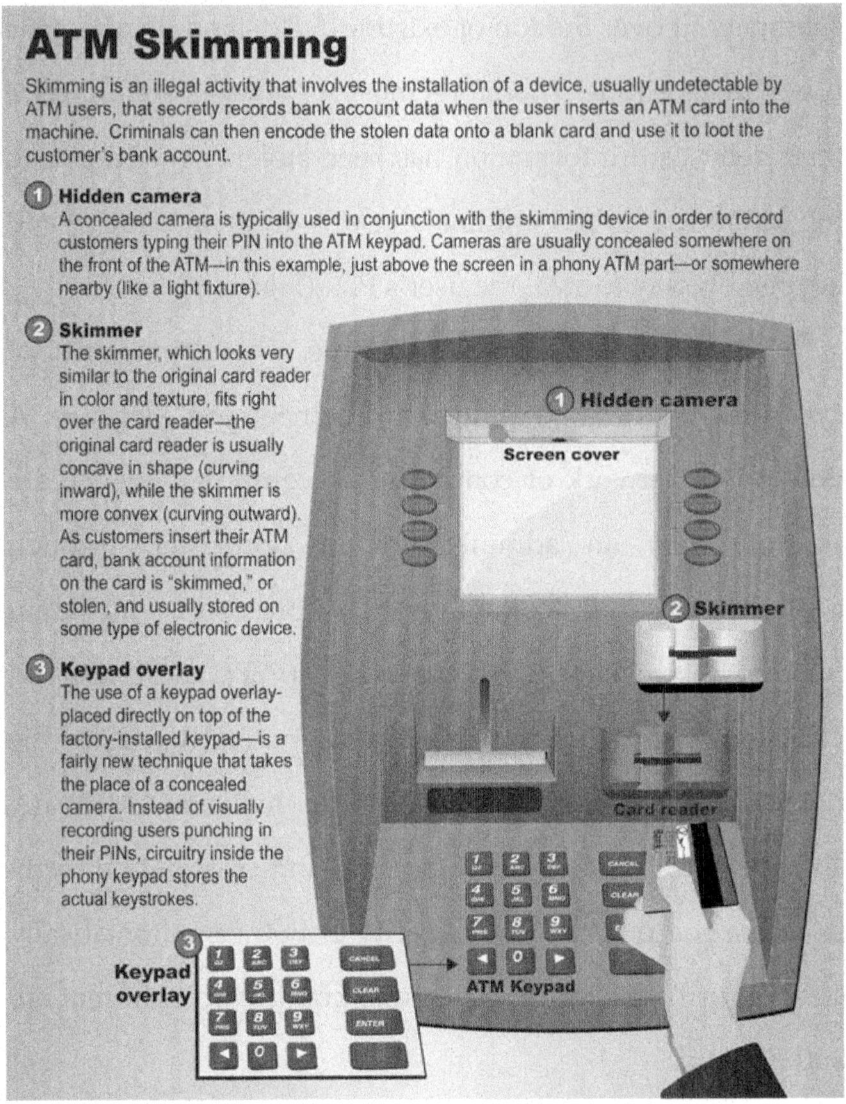

ATM Skimming

Skimming is an illegal activity that involves the installation of a device, usually undetectable by ATM users, that secretly records bank account data when the user inserts an ATM card into the machine. Criminals can then encode the stolen data onto a blank card and use it to loot the customer's bank account.

① Hidden camera

A concealed camera is typically used in conjunction with the skimming device in order to record customers typing their PIN into the ATM keypad. Cameras are usually concealed somewhere on the front of the ATM—in this example, just above the screen in a phony ATM part—or somewhere nearby (like a light fixture).

② Skimmer

The skimmer, which looks very similar to the original card reader in color and texture, fits right over the card reader—the original card reader is usually concave in shape (curving inward), while the skimmer is more convex (curving outward). As customers insert their ATM card, bank account information on the card is "skimmed," or stolen, and usually stored on some type of electronic device.

③ Keypad overlay

The use of a keypad overlay-placed directly on top of the factory-installed keypad—is a fairly new technique that takes the place of a concealed camera. Instead of visually recording users punching in their PINs, circuitry inside the phony keypad stores the actual keystrokes.

① Hidden camera

Screen cover

② Skimmer

Card reader

③ Keypad overlay

ATM Keypad

Figure 6. An FBI breakdown of how ATM Skimming works. (Source: www.fbi.gov)

Russian and Balkan cyber criminals operate many of the most advanced botnets, including the Game Over Zeus Botnet [6]. The FBI estimates that the Game Over Zeus

Botnet is responsible for over $100 million in losses [3]. Botnets are further discussed in Chapter 4, Vulnerabilities and Exploits.

The fact many hackers operate out of Russia and Eastern Europe is no coincidence. Most of the countries have limited or no hacking laws and are largely unwilling to cooperate with foreign law enforcement against their own citizens. Security researchers have confirmed that the malware used in both the Target and Home Depot attacks originated in Russia and is likely the work of a Ukrainian hacker [7]. So, as long as these hackers do not attack anything within their own country, they operate with impunity [8].

This has led to the heavy involvement of Russian organized crime in hacking and credit card fraud. According to some reports, Russian organized crime has stolen over 1.2 billion usernames and passwords from 400,000 websites [9]. Often the hacking is secretly sponsored by the Russian government, and the hackers know they are insulated from prosecution [8].

What began as an expression of curiosity and a quest for knowledge has become one of the most lucrative crimes in the world. Cybercrime or hacking is now estimated to cost between $375 to $570 billion annually [10]. Furthermore, the ability to commit cybercrime from anywhere in the world and out of reach of many law enforcement agencies, has led to many criminal organizations committing cybercrime.

Chapter References

[1] (Wallace & Erickson, 1992)

[2] (EC-Council, 2014; ISC2, 2014)

[3] (FBI, 2014)

[4] (Taylor, Fritsch, & Liederback, 2014)

[5] (Wang & Yu, 2009)

[6] (Alhomoud et al., 2013)

[7] (Gumuchian & Goldman, 2014)

[8] (Risen, 2014; Shuster, 2010)

[9] (Siciliano, 2014)

[10] (McAfee, 2014)

4

VULNERABILITIES AND EXPLOITS

Whether cybercrime is committed by a hacker, a criminal organization, an intelligence agency or a military service, the same underlying techniques, tactics, and procedures are used to commit the crime. Either an insider has to knowingly or unknowingly, provide access to an information system. Or, there must be a vulnerability in the information system that can be exploited. This chapter explores the different vulnerabilities and exploits used to commit cybercrime.

Probably the simplest vulnerability that is exploited to

commit cybercrime is people. In terms of cybercrime, exploiting people is referred to as social engineering. The goal of social engineering is to exploit, i.e. "trick" people into providing access to an information system. The access can be obtained many ways, but most often it involves sending phishing emails or convincing someone to give you access.

In the first type of phishing emails, a hacker sends an email to a victim and tries to trick the victim into entering their username and password for a website. This social engineering technique is called phishing because the hacker sends hundreds or thousands of email message and hopes to "hook" one victim. The emails are made to appear they have been sent from a bank, financial institution, email provider, eBay, Facebook, or any type of online service that requires a username and password. The email contains a link to a website that will mirror the legitimate website, but when the user enters their username and password, the hacker captures the login credentials. The hacker can then use the login and password to steal money, order credit cards, or send spam email messages.

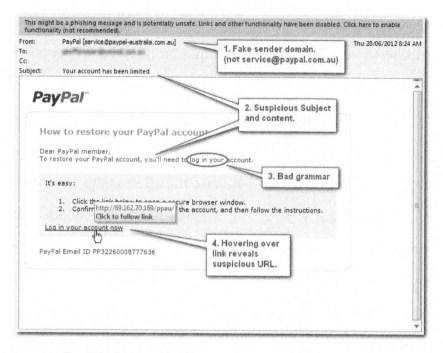

Figure 7. PayPal Phishing Email.

The second type of social engineering also involves an email message and a hyperlink to a webpage, but rather than trying to capture the username and password, the hyperlink takes the victim to a website that contains malicious code. This type of attack is called a "drive by download." According to Niels Provos of the Google Security Team: "A drive by download exploits a vulnerability in the browser to execute a malicious program on a user's computer without their knowledge."[1] Once the malicious code (Malware) is executed on the victim's computer, the hacker can send spam messages, steal login credentials, credit card numbers, and personally identifiable information (PII) that are entered in the browser.

This type of phishing email can also have the malicious software attached directly to the email message. If the victim runs the malicious software the effect is the same as if the victim had visited the website and downloaded it manually. The malicious attachments can be many different types of files from executables (.exe) to Microsoft Office files (.doc, .xls), and Adobe (.pdf) files. Most executable files are blocked by email providers, therefore office documents with malicious macros are very common and so are PDF files with bound executables.

The final social engineering scenario involves direct victim contact by the criminal, either in person or via the telephone. This scenario is very simple. The criminal tries to trick the victim into providing them their username and password. Criminals often pose as IT help desk personnel or technicians and will use information obtained from the internet about the company to put the victim at ease.

When hackers aren't exploiting people, they are exploiting vulnerabilities in information systems. These vulnerabilities can exist in many different types of software and hardware. But they are too numerous to cover entirely, so we will focus on the most prevalent vulnerabilities. SQL injection is by far the most used attack on the internet [2]. The SANS institute and MITRE also ranked SQL injection as the top threat, with Operating System Command injection and Cross-site scripting (XSS) the next most prevalent attack techniques [3].

A SQL injection attack: "consists of insertion or 'injection' of a SQL query via the input data from the client to the application" [4]. The majority of SQL injection attacks are targeted at webservers and the databases behind the webservers. Many SQL injection attacks target PHP and ASP applications on webservers [4]. Hackers use a data entry field on a webpage to insert or "inject" SQL statements into the database. For example, in the login and password fields on a website, an attacker is able to insert ' OR "=' into the two fields. This may log you in as the first user in the database, which in the example below is Jake. Different SQL statements and injections can allow the attacker to read sensitive data, modify data, or execute administrative commands on the database.

So what does this mean for you, and why should you care about SQL injection attacks? Whenever you enter your information on an ecommerce website, it is usually stored in a SQL database. So when the hackers attack the SQL database they are able to download the tables from the database. Stored in these tables is your information, including credit card numbers, email addresses, and your address.

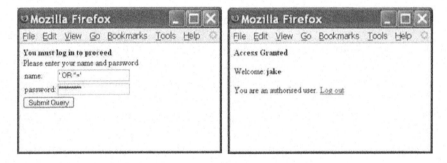

Figure 8. SQL Injection

The second most prevalent attack technique on webservers is cross-site scripting (XSS). XSS is another form of injection attack, however the technique sends scripts instead of SQL statements in data fields to compromise a website. The scripts entered in the data fields are executed on the website. The scripts can also be stored on the website and ran against the next person to access the website. The damage can range from a simple popup window, to stealing login credentials or cookies [4]. The example below shows a XSS attack which executes the script and causes a popup on the webserver.

While the popup is a simple example, more complex XSS attacks capture the data you enter in the fields and sends it to the hacker. So, when you enter your credit card number, or email address and password, the hacker obtains a copy.

Figure 9. Cross Site Scripting (XSS)

Any discussion on cybercrime techniques would not be complete without mentioning Botnets and Distributed Denial of Service Attacks. Botnets are thousands of compromised computers that are remotely controlled by a Botmaster. The computers were originally compromised with malware that allows the Botmaster to perform different malicious activities on the computer. These malicious activities include stealing usernames and passwords, sending spam email, or executing distributed denial of service attacks. The Botmaster has the option of controlling a single computer, a group of computers, or the entire botnet.

The size and scope of botnets are hard to imagine. In February 2010, Spanish authorities and the FBI dismantled the Mariposa botnet, which consisted of over 12 million compromised computers [5]. Only two years after the takedown of the Mariposa botnet, another botnet, the Metulji botnet, was dismantled by the FBI and consisted of over 20 million compromised computers [6]. Then in March, 2012, Microsoft and the Financial Services Information Sharing and Analysis Center helped dismantle the family of Zeus botnets in response to over 13 million Zeus botnet infections worldwide[7].

One of the biggest threats from botnets is their ability to execute large distributed denial of service (DDOS) attacks. During a DDOS attack, all the botnet computers send thousands of internet packets at a single webserver and overwhelm the webserver. The objective of the DDOS attack is to render the webserver unable to respond to legitimate requests. In March 2013, the Spamhaus Project, a nonprofit organization that tracks email spam sources, was attacked with a distributed denial of service attack that exceeded 300

Gigabits per second, the largest distributed denial of service attack ever observed at that time [8].

As part of my doctoral dissertation, I constructed a simple *Dark DDoser* botnet in a virtual environment. During a DDOS attack in the lab, the *Dark DDoser* Botnet sent a total of 108,496 SYN packets in 159 seconds. Since the *Dark DDoser* botnet was comprised of only three computers, the average rate of attack packets was over 227 packets per second by each computer. In a real DDOS attack, these packet rates would easily overwhelm a small webserver.

As you can see in the *Dark DDoSer* command and control shell below, the Botmaster has a listing of bots (compromised computers) that are currently connected to the internet and communicating with the Botmaster's command and control server. In this example there are 6 bots, 3 from the United States, and one each from Ireland, Great Britain, and Italy. Since this botnet is specially designed to launch distributed denial of service attacks, the DDOS launching command is front and center. In the field labelled IP Address, you enter the IP address of the computer you want to attack and click the send command. All the bots on the screen will then start to send thousands of packets to the victim computer. While the DDOS attack is ongoing the victim computer is overwhelmed and is not able to respond to legitimate Internet connections, or connect to web sites.

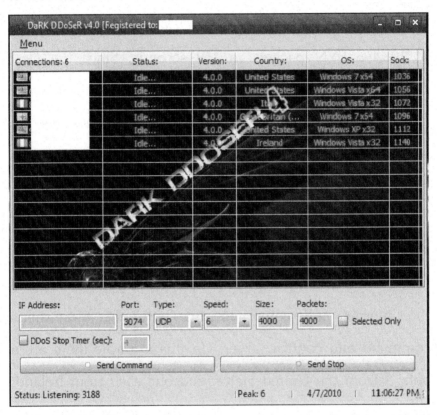

Figure 10. Dark DDoSer Botnet Command and Control Shell

The ease of use and number of vulnerable computers on the internet has led to a surge in botnets and DDOS attacks. As you will read in the chapter on the Deep Web and the Cyber Underground, the underground hacker forums are full of advertisements for botnet malware, compromised computers, and DDOS attacks for purchase.

Chapter References

[1] (Provos, 2012)

[2] (Curtis, 2012)

[3] (SANS & MITRE, 2011)

[4] (OWASP, 2014)

[5] (Roscini, 2014)

[6] (Ventre, 2013)

[7] (Alhomoud, Awan, Disso, & Younas, 2013)

[8] (Fachkha, Bou-Hard, & Debbabi, 2013)

5

CYBER-TERRORISM

Cyber terrorism is a highly publicized subject and much research has been conducted on the topic. A search on Google scholar for the term cyber terrorism returns over 62,000 hits on journal articles, books, and reports, while a general Google search returns over 4 million hits. However, at the time this book was written, not one person has been physically harmed by cyber terrorism [1]. This begs the question: What is the actual threat of cyber terrorism? This chapter looks at the history of cyber terrorism, reviews past examples of cyber terrorism, analyzes the current threat of cyber terrorism, and also examines the use of the internet and technology by terrorist organizations.

There are many definitions of terrorism, and they all include the threat of, or actual use of force or violence, to intimidate or coerce persons or governments in furtherance of the terrorist organizations objectives [2]. A logical definition of cyber terrorism would be: an act of terrorism carried out primarily via cyber means, i.e. through computers and the internet. Obviously, afflicting direct violence to a person through the internet or via a computer is very difficult, however it is not impossible. The simplest means is through medical devices controlled by computers that are connected to a person as well as the internet. If a terrorist could access the medical device via the internet and effect its operation, they may injure or kill the patient.

More sophisticated cyber terrorism attacks may target critical infrastructure that people really on for basic life support, such as public water systems and electrical distribution systems. If the infrastructure was affected long enough, the health or life of people could be at risk. The threat of such attacks are very frightening for people and although there are very few examples of actual cyber terrorism attacks, the topic is widely covered in the media and discussed by politicians.

While not violent or casualty producing, attacks on webservers and network devices still produce media coverage and allow terrorist organizations to claim attribution for the attack, spread propaganda, and induce fear of larger, more sophisticated attacks. Examples of these attacks are denial of service attacks and web defacements. The 2007 cyber-attack on Estonia is an example of damage that can be caused by cyber terrorism. During the cyber-attack on Estonia, government websites, news media sites, and online banking sites were all attacked with distributed denial of service attacks and taken offline [3]. While this attack is not attributed to a terrorist organization, a similar attack could be, and the resulting news stories and media coverage would enable a terrorist organization to install fear in a population and threaten future attacks.

The first report of cyber terrorism occurred in 1996 when a white supremacist organization attacked an internet service provider that tried to stop the organization from sending racist email messages [4]. The cyber-attack damaged the ISPs record keeping system and the terrorist left a message to the ISP stating they have not yet seen true electronic terrorism [4].

A more widely publicized cyber-terrorism attack occurred in 1998, when the terrorist organization, the Tamil Tigers attacked the Sri Lankan Embassies with massive amounts of email messages for over two weeks [5]. This was an attempt to disrupt the communication abilities of the Sri Lankan government. Also in 1998, the Irish Republican Army hired hackers to steal the home addresses of British law enforcement and intelligence officers from government computers [5].

Since the turn of the century there have been numerous reports of terrorist's using the internet to further their agenda with recruiting, fundraising, and spreading propaganda. According to Theohary and Rollins (2011), cybercrime has surpassed drug trafficking as the top fundraising activity for terrorist organizations [6]. For example, Al-Queda has used credit card fraud and identity theft to finance terrorist activities [7]. The Revolutionary Armed Forces of Colombia (FARC) maintain an elaborate website to spread their ideology and provide information on a variety of subjects affecting Columbia [8].

On January 12, 2014, the Twitter account of U.S. Central Command was compromised and messages supporting the Islamic State of Iraq and Syria (ISIS) were posted on the Twitter account. Below are three messages posted by ISIS on the CECNTCOM Twitter account.

AMERICAN SOLDIERS, WE ARE COMING, WATCH YOUR BACK. ISIS. http://t.co/iZULe4nTmp #CyberCaliphate
— U.S. Central Command (@CENTCOM) January 12, 2015

We won't stop! We know everything about you, your wives and children. pic.twitter.com/ixz82lCDES
— U.S. Central Command (@CENTCOM) January 12, 2015

ISIS is already here, we are in your PCs, in each military base. pic.twitter.com/xafTqTMvN5
— U.S. Central Command (@CENTCOM) January 12, 2015

As would be expected, these messages were highly publicized in the media and American service members and their families may have been concerned about their safety.

ISIS was able to embarrass the United States, gain wide spread media coverage for the hack, and spread their message and propaganda.

The FBI believes terrorist originations will conduct cyberattacks in coordination with conventional terrorist attacks, as well attempt cyberattacks against the critical infrastructure of the United States [9]. Even if a cyberattack was not fully successful, the publicity from an attack on the critical infrastructure would still have the desired effect, fear amongst the population. Weimann predicts terrorists will increasingly turn to cyberterrorism and as their technological capabilities increase, the threat of cyberterrorism will continue to rise [10].

Chapter References

[1] (Singer & Friedman, 2014)

[2] (Federal Bureau of Investigation, 2010; Annual Country Reports on Terrorism, 2011)

[3] line (Arimateia da Cruz, 2013)

[4] (Easttom & Taylor, 2011)

[5] (Denning, 2000)

[6] (Theohary & Rollins, 2011)

[7] (Rollins & Wilson, 2007)

[8] (Weimann, 2006)

[9] (Chabinsky, 2009)

[10] (Weimann, 2004)

6

INFORMATION WARFARE

There have been wars as long as Man has been alive. Many of the technology advances throughout history have been a result of war and the search for the next great weapon or military communication system. In 1969, with the launch of ARPANET and the development of packet switched networks, the world started down a new path of digital communications and information sharing. Over the last 45 years, the ARPANET grew to what we now know as the Internet.

Also during this time, the governments and militaries of

the world began to rely heavily on computers and networks, both wired and wireless, for communications, and command and control of the military and their weapon systems. As a result, the computers and networks are seen as possible targets during war and armed conflict. In March 2014, Vice Admiral Michael Rodgers testified before Congress that the US Military's ground troops would soon have dedicated forces to conduct cyber-attacks.

In 2008 during the war between Russia and Georgia, we saw a small portion of Russia's information warfare capabilities. Georgian government websites, and news media websites were systematically attacked with large distributed denial of service attacks [1]. As a result, the Georgian government was unable to react publically during the war and the Georgian population was restricted in the news they were able to obtain [1]. The lack of information and inability of the Georgian population to receive news updates from their government spread fear and animosity.

During the 2014 invasion of Crimea, Ukraine and subsequent annexation by Russia, we again saw the information warfare capabilities of Russia. Although not as severe as during the war with Georgia, Russia again used a distributed denial of service attack to disabled the servers of Ukraine's National Security and Defense Council [2].

But it is not just Russia that conducts information warfare. In August 2012, Saudi Arabia's National Oil Company (Aramco) was attacked by the Shamoon malware which wipes the hard drives of its victim computers [3]. During the attack over 30,000 computers were infected and their hard drives wiped. It is believed Iran was behind the attack on Aramco [3].

In November 2014, the FBI said North Korea hacked Sony Pictures Entertainment in response to the Sony movie, The Interview, where the plot is to kill the leader of North Korea. But Sony wasn't attacked with a distributed denial of service attack, Sony was the victim of a full computer intrusion and exfiltration of sensitive data. The attackers also destroyed data and erased hard drives on Sony's servers. Subsequently, the hackers released internal communications and employee details in an attempt to embarrass and intimidate Sony. In response to the attack, the United States Government passed sanctions on ten North Korean officials and three North Korean Government agencies [4].

The troubling aspect of the Aramco and Sony attacks are

the physical damage that was done to the victim's computer. Historically hackers, cyber criminals and nations compromised computers to gather intelligence or steal information. However, both the Aramco and Sony attacks went a step further and deliberately wiped hard drives and destroyed data. General Keith Alexander, the former head of the NSA and Commander of the U.S. Cyber Command told the Australian Financial Review:

"The new age was not necessarily Stuxnet. It was what happened to Saudi Aramco in August 2012. That's the wakeup call, I think, for everybody. DDOS attackers employed a virus that infected the hard drives of over 30,000 computers at Aramco, overwriting and effectively destroying data. A similar attack on our critical infrastructure networks could have grave effects on financial markets, communication networks, and health and safety services to name a few" [5].

During an armed conflict, information warfare is now a standard operating procedure for militaries. However, covert attacks undertaken outside of an armed conflict are considered a gray between an act of war and an intelligence operation. The 2010 Kaspersky Lab report of the Stuxnet worm shows the advanced nature of information warfare, and how such activities can be considered acts of war or intelligence activities depending on your perspective.

Stuxnet is a worm that was specifically designed to attack Windows computers that were running Siemens Step 7 software [6]. Siemens Step 7 software is used to operate SCADA systems and programmable logic controls (PLC), and it just so happens that the Iranian nuclear plants use Siemens Step 7 software to operate their centrifuges.

However, the Iranian nuclear plant's computers that operate the centrifuges are not connected to the Internet [6]. So Stuxnet was designed to spread via USB infection. Thus, if an Iranian scientist's home computer was infected, and they used the same USB flash drive at home and at work, Stuxnet would be spread to the work computer. Once infected the computers reported false information, that the centrifuges were operating properly, while the centrifuges were actually spinning too fast and destroyed themselves [6]. A very important aspect of Stuxnet, although it would spread to any Windows computer available, it would only perform malicious activities on computers with Siemens Step 7 software and operating centrifuges [7]. Therefore, it appears Stuxnet was developed specifically to target Iran's nuclear program and affect its centrifuges.

From the Iranian government's perspective, they may consider the use of Stuxnet to destroy its centrifuges an act of war. But Iran is unable to say for certain which country, organization or persons perpetrated the attack. So how can they respond, if the attacker is unknown.

On the other hand, the country that developed Stuxnet and attacked the Iranian centrifuges would argue the attack was espionage, meant to delay the development of the Iranian nuclear program and thus, not an act of war.

The question of attribution is very important when discussing information warfare because it is not always possible to determine which country committed an act. Information warfare has a short history, and the rules governing what constitutes an act of war are not clearly defined for information warfare. Do these new proactive measures constitute an act of war? Are state sponsored cyber-attacks different than a conventional attack?

The United Nations Charter deals with warfare and use of force between states. Article 2, Section 4 states: "All Members shall refrain in their international relations from the threat or use of force against the territorial integrity or political independence of any state, or in any other manner inconsistent with the Purposes of the United Nations" [8].

The United Nations Security Council also deals with use of force and acts of war. U.N. Charter, Article 39 states:

"The Security Council shall determine the existence of any threat to the peace, breach of the peace, or act of aggression and shall make recommendations, or decide what measures shall be taken in accordance with Articles 41 and 42, to maintain or restore international peace and security" [8].

Article 42 states:

"Should the Security Council consider that measures provided for in Article 41 would be inadequate or have proved to be inadequate, it may take such action by air, sea, or land forces as may be necessary to maintain or restore international peace and security. Such action may include demonstrations, blockade, and other operations by air, sea, or land forces of Members of the United Nations" [8].

And finally, Article 51 states:

"Nothing in the present Charter shall impair the inherent right of individual or collective self-defense if an armed attack occurs against a Member of the United Nations, until the Security Council has taken measures necessary to maintain international peace and security. Measures taken by Members in the exercise of this right of self-defense shall be immediately reported to the Security Council and shall not in any way affect the authority and responsibility of the Security Council under the present Charter to take at any time such action as it deems necessary in order to maintain or restore international peace and security" [8].

Under these articles, it is clear Nations' have a right of self-defense if attacked. So what about information warfare attacks? This goes back to the earlier question of attribution. It is very difficult to say with absolute certainty that one country was responsible for a cyber-attack. Thus, it is difficult to respond to such an attack. Finally, consider this question: If a Nation is attacked with a cyber-attack, can that Nation then respond in defense with a conventional attack? While this has not happened yet, there may be a day when militaries respond to cyber-attacks with traditional physical attacks, such as missiles or bombs.

Chapter References

[1] (Hollis, 2008)

[2] (Matlack, 2014)

[3] (Viswanatha & Menn, 2015)

[4] (Kim & Lerman, 2015)

[5] (Joye, 2014)

[6] (Kushner, 2014)

[7] (Zetter, 2011)

[8] (United Nations, 1945)

7

CYBER ESPIONAGE

Cyber Espionage is a relatively new technique in the long history of intelligence gathering and espionage. The ARPANET was developed in 1969, so at most cyber espionage is only 45 years old [1]. However, in the last 20 years, cyber espionage has grown rapidly. In response to the threat, Congress passed the Economic Espionage Act of 1996, which makes it a crime to steal trade secrets to benefit any foreign government, or to benefit any person other than the owner of the trade secret. These laws are codified in 18 U.S.C., Section 1831, and Section 1832 [2].

Recent news reports and Government press releases show the growing threat of cyber espionage. Most governments and large corporations are likely to face cyber espionage threats from foreign governments and industrial competitors.

On May 19, 2014, the United States Department of Justice took the unusual step of indicting five Chinese military hackers for cyber espionage [3]. It is interesting to note, the five were not indicted for hacking government computers, but rather private industry. The victims included Westinghouse, U.S. subsidiaries of SolarWorld AG, United States Steel Corporation, Allegheny Technologies Inc. (ATI), the United Steel, Paper and Forestry, Rubber, Manufacturing, Energy, Allied Industrial and Service Workers International Union and Alcoa [3]. This should raise the awareness level of all information security professionals because it shows the government is not the only target, but that private industry is a target of cyber espionage as well.

While China garners all the attention of the media, there are many countries conducting cyber espionage, including the United States. The mission of the National Security

Agency is, "collects, processes, and disseminates intelligence information from foreign signals for intelligence and counterintelligence purposes and to support military operations"[4].

The Economist (2014) believes that in addition to China, Russia, and America, many other countries including Pakistan, North Korea, and even some African countries are committing cyber espionage [10]. The low cost of cyber espionage, as compared to traditional espionage, means many more countries can afford to conduct espionage via a cyber technique. There are reports of Iran, Syria, Israel, Cuba, Venezuela, Brazil, and many others committing cyber espionage.

If you think about state sponsored cyber espionage in purely monetary figures, it is much cheaper to train a group of government hackers, then to design a stealth aircraft. The government hackers can then steal stealth aircraft designs from another country, and the savings are astronomical. Furthermore, the cost savings continue after the theft because once the government hackers are trained they will continue to steal other designs and trade secrets.

The most detailed account of cyber espionage to date is

described in Mandiant's 2013 report, "APT1: Exposing One of China's Cyber Espionage Units" [5]. Mandiant is an cyber incident response company. From 2006 through 2013, they responded to 141 computer intrusions which they believe are all related. Mandiant reports all 141 intrusion are the work of a single Chinese Intelligence Organization, Unit 61398. The report detailed the methodology, techniques, and tactics used by Unit 61398 to infiltrate these companies and steal hundreds of terabytes of data [5]. The term advanced persistent threat (APT) is used to describe these attacks because the attackers are relentless and will continue to try different attacks and exploits until they are successful. No industry is exempt from these attacks. APT1 included 20 different industries, in 15 countries [5].

While the theft of trade secrets is a serious threat, it is not the only threat from cyber espionage. Cyber espionage also targets raw intelligence of foreign governments and militaries. Edward Snowden disclosed many classified programs the United States Government used to collect intelligence via cyber espionage [6]. The media made these revelations seem shocking and asked the question: why would America do this? But, as was written above, it is the mission of the NSA to collect signal and cyber intelligence. Why is anyone surprised that the NSA is actually doing its job?

Governments not only collect intelligence through cyber espionage, they also use court orders to obtain data on individuals from private corporations. In response to the number of government requests for data and the revelations reveled by Edward Snowden on U.S. Government intelligence collection, many corporations will now notify the customer whenever the government requires them to provide customer data [7]. This change in customer notification policy includes Microsoft, Yahoo, Facebook, Twitter, Google, and Apple. The ironic aspect of this change is the vast amount of information private companies collect on their customers.

Take Google for example. Google not only saves all the search queries of customers, they also scan all your Gmail [8]. Even more alarming, Google also scans all emails sent to, or from, a Gmail user from a non-Gmail account [8].

But, the most invasive aspect of Google's data collection is the GPS location data they maintain. If you have an Android cellular phone, or have installed Google Maps on a non-Android phone, Google records your GPS location. If you go to the website, https://maps.google.com/ locationhistory/b/0, and log into your Google account, you can see the information Google has collected. It is troublesome that a private company knows your location on any given day and time, as well as your travel patterns.

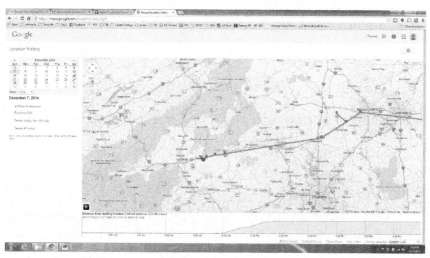

Figure 10. Google location history

Above is an example of the aforementioned Google location history. This shows my location during a trip from Raleigh to the North Carolina mountains.

In addition to Google, Apple also collects and maintains your location information. And these were two of the most vocal companies about government data collection.

A recent report by Symantec detailed a newly

discovered piece of malware, Regin, designed to spy on governments and industry in European and Asian countries [9]. According to Symantec:

"Regin is a highly-complex threat which has been used in systematic data collection or intelligence gathering campaigns. The development and operation of this malware would have required a significant investment of time and resources, indicating that a nation state is responsible. Its design makes it highly suited for persistent, long term surveillance operations against targets" [9].

"The discovery of Regin highlights how significant investments continue to be made into the development of tools for use in intelligence gathering" [9].

The threat of cyber espionage is rapidly increasing and the low cost of entry for nation-states is compounding the threat. The threat includes the theft of trade secrets, as well as intelligence collection. Information security and assurance professionals are likely to face serious threats from cyber espionage across a majority of industries and government sectors. The threat is so severe, that Russia recently ordered 20 typewriters [10].

Furthermore, the United States military continues to use technologies from the 1960s and '70s within their nuclear missile silos to mitigate the threat of cyber espionage and hacking [11]. By using 8 inch floppy drives and analog phones, and not being connected to the internet, the nuclear missiles are secure from hackers and foreign governments [11].

Chapter References

[1] (Waldrop, 2008)

[2] (FBI, 2014)

[3] (DOJ, 2014)

[4] (NSA, 2014)

[5] (Mandiant, 2013)

[6] (Franceshi-Bicchierai, 2014)

[7] (Gokey, 2014)

[8] (Gillmor, 2014)

[9] (Symantec, 2014)

[10] (Economist, 2014)

[11] (McCaney, 2014)

8

HACKTIVISM

In recent years, a new form of activism has emerged, which combines traditional activism and hacking. *Hacktivism*, as the new online activism has been called, is a decentralized set of individuals who target governments, corporations, politicians, and anyone or anything that challenges the collective beliefs of the group.

Hacktivist do not operate as a set group of members, but rather, they are all individuals who come together online when an event motivates them to respond. Often, individuals of different ideological backgrounds will temporarily work together to challenge what both see as an injustice.

The term hacktivist was developed in 1996 by a computer hacker nicknamed, Omega, who is a long time member of the infamous hacking group, the Cult of the Dead Cow [1]. Omega and other members of the Cult of the Dead Cow saw a hacktivist as a hacker who was politically motivated. The original acts of hacktivists are traced to nuclear disarmament in 1989 [2].

Although hacktivists have been around for many years, it was not until 2010 that hacktivists gained wide spread notoriety. In 2010, Bradley Manning, a private in the U.S. Army, stole thousands of classified documents, videos, and diplomatic cables, and provided them to Julian Assange of WikiLeaks. Assange then published the information on the WikiLeaks website [3].

In response to the posting and pressure from the United States government, many companies including Amazon, PayPal, Visa, MasterCard, and Bank of America cancelled accounts associated with WikiLeaks [4]. As a result of these actions, hacktivists immediately started a campaign against the companies [4]. The most notorious hacktivist group,

Anonymous, launched Operation Payback, which consisted of distributed denial of service attacks against the companies. The wide spread media coverage of the WikiLeaks release of classified information and subsequent DDoS attacks by Anonymous brought hacktivism to minds of the public.

The news coverage and social media response also provided Anonymous and other hacktivists with recruiting and propaganda platforms. Combined with increased internet connectivity around the world, hacktivists were able to create armies of cyber soldiers. The anonymity with which hacktivists operate, and little fear of retribution inspired many people to conduct hacktivism with groups such as Anonymous. As the hacktivist attacks grew and generated increased new coverage, the group Anonymous became known worldwide. So much so, that the Guy Fawkes mask is now synonymous with the group Anonymous.

Figure 11. Guy Fawkes Mask

However, hacktivists such as Anonymous, also caught the attention of law enforcement. In June, 2011, 16 members of Anonymous were arrested by the FBI for the DDoS attack on PayPal [5]. Another hacktivist group, LulzSec, was charged with hacking the Sony PlayStation Store, PBS, and Fox News in 2011 [6].

But the arrest of its members did not stop Anonymous. In 2011 and 2012, Anonymous and other hacktivists attacked Middle Eastern governments during the Arab Spring in response to the governments' crack down on protestors [2].

Also in 2012, Anonymous responded to the take down of the file sharing website, Megaupload.com, by asking people to download the Low Orbit Ion Cannon (LOIC), a DoS tool and help the hacktivist group launch attacks. The Low Orbit Ion Cannon is a simple program that allows a computer to launch a denial of service attack by sending thousands of network packets a minute. As a result of Anonymous' request, thousands of people installed the LOIC and participated in the hacktivist attack against the Department of Justice, RIAA, and MPAA [7]. Unfortunately for many of the hacktivists who installed and used the LIOC, the LIOC does not mask your IP address and some of the hacktivists were identified and arrested. Like a game of cops and robbers, the FBI again made high profile arrests of five Anonymous members in March of 2012 [8].

There are many other examples of hacktivism and most involve DDoS attacks against government agencies and large corporations. But some hacktivist operations include releasing personal or embarrassing information of individuals, often politicians or government officials. The collective of hacktivists, including Anonymous, are a loosely organized group of individuals who come together to fight what they view as injustices. The internet has allowed hacktivists to exist and the internet is the primary tool of hacktivists.

Chapter References

[1] (Mills, 2012)

[2] (Paganini, 2013)

[3] (Simpson & Roshan, 2013)

[4] (Hampson, 2012)

[5] (Millis, 2011)

[6] (Arthur, 2013)

[7] (Greenberg, 2012)

[8] (FBI, 2012)

9

CYBER UNDERGROUND, THE DEEP WEB, AND

HACKER FORUMS

When most people refer to the Internet, they are actually describing the World Wide Web (Web). The Web consists of the hypertext documents accessible via web browsers such as Internet Explorer, Chrome, and Firefox. But, the Web is actually just one of many avenues for transmitting and receiving data on the Internet. In addition to Web, there is electronic mail, File Transfer Protocol (FTP), Telnet, Usenet bulletin boards, Internet Relay Chat (IRC), Gopher, secure shell (SSH), and many more applications that use the

Internet, not the World Wide Web. To understand the Cyber Underground and its depth, we first have to review the Internet as a whole.

On October 29, 1969, the ARPANET became the first operational packet switched networked. Prior to the ARPANET, networks used circuit switched networks. The most well-known circuit switched network is the traditional land line telephone network.

Imagine the days when an operator would connect two telephones on the switch board. What the operators were actually doing was connecting the circuits between the two phones. During the length of that specific telephone call, the circuit was dedicated exclusively to its duration, and could not be used by any other telephones. A good example of a circuit not being available is the busy signal on the telephone. When you tried to call a telephone and the circuit was in use, you received a signal identifying that the circuit was not available. Many people will also recall the recording when attempting to make a telephone call, "all circuits are busy now, please try your call again later." This highlights the pitfalls of circuit switching, there are only so many available circuits and if all the circuits are in use, no resources can communicate until a circuit becomes available.

Figure 12. Circuit Switch Board. (Source: www.jber.af.mil)

The ARPANET introduced the concept of a packet switched network, where data is split into small "packets" and sent individually. When the packets are received at their destination, they are reassembled to form the original data.

The advantage of packet switching is many hosts, i.e. computers or telephones, can share a network at the same time by interspersing the small packets on the network. The other advantage of packet switched networks is routing. Unlike dedicated circuits that use a dedicated route (or line) for the connection, the individual packets sent on packet switched networks can take any available route to reach their destination.

From 1969 until 1989, the Internet consisted of mainframe computers, servers, and personal computers that communicated on the internet via electronic mail, bulletin boards, newsgroups, and shared data and files between themselves. Then, Tim Bernes-Lee and Robert Cailliau developed the concept of the World Wide Web and Hypertext in 1989 [1]. Shortly thereafter, the first commercial web browser Mosaic was developed, and web pages began to populate the World Wide Web.

The World Wide Web today consists of the webpages and data that are retrievable via a web browser such as Internet Explorer, Safari or Chrome. Domain names make browsing websites easy and user friendly. Since a unique name is registered with the domain name system (DNS) for every website, there is no need to remember an Internet Protocol (IP) address for the website. The invention of the World Wide Web and the domain name system make the use of the Internet an everyday accessibility for billions of people.

While the majority of the world thinks the World Wide

Web is the Internet; the Internet that existed before the invention of the World Wide Web is still alive and well today. This is what many people refer to as the Deep Web or the Cyber Underground, and includes bulletin boards, databases, chat servers, FTP file servers, and legacy systems.

The Deep Web also consists of dynamic web pages and websites that are not accessible via normal web browsers or IP addresses. The Deep Web is not indexed by popular search engines such as Google, Bing, or Yahoo; so the Deep Web is not searchable by normal World Wide Web applications. Rather, users must use special software to reach the Deep Web and view the content.

One of the most popular software for viewing portions of the Deep Web is TOR, i.e., The Onion Router. TOR is a program you can run on your computer that helps keep you safe on the Internet. TOR protects you by bouncing your communications around a distributed network of relays run by volunteers all around the world: it prevents somebody watching your Internet connection from learning what sites you visit, and it prevents the sites you visit from learning your IP address and physical location [2].

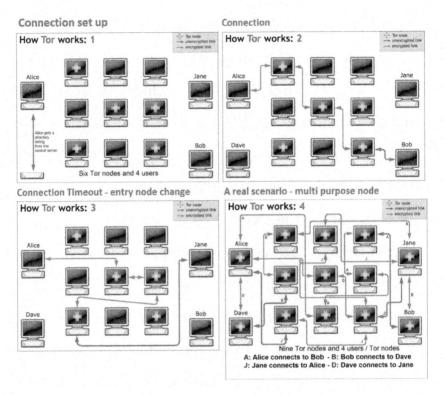

Figure 13. How Tor Works. (Source: www.securityaffairs.co)

But TOR also provides access to websites ending in the domain suffix, .onion. These websites are not accessible via normal web browsers and the location of the web hosting server, and system administrator are unknown. This providers hackers and criminals the ability to hide their identities and sell contraband with impunity.

In addition to the Deep Web, there is also the Darknet. Similar to peer-to-peer networks (P2P), but the Darknet consists of private networks that only trusted peers can connect to, whereas P2P networks allow anyone to connect [3]. The Darknet also uses non-standard protocols and ports to communicate across the Internet to help avoid detection. Popular Darknet software includes Freenet, GNUnet and Retroshare.

Last but not least are the cyber forums. Cyber forums are websites where hackers and cyber criminals discuss hacking, and buy or sell hacking tools, compromised accounts, stolen credit cards, botnets and distributed denial of service attacks. Many of the cyber forums are visible to anyone on the Internet, but some are password protected and require an invitation to participate in the forum. A Google search for hacker forums returns over 11 million results. An online Marketplace that is part of a cyber forum for hackers is shown below and the number of posts is over 3 million.

Figure 14. Hacker Forum Online Marketplace

Within the Marketplace compromised computers sell for as little as 20 cents apiece, DDOS attacks sell for $15 per month for unlimited attacks, and malware to setup your own botnet is only $19.99.

Figure 15. Compromised Computers for Sale

Figure 16. Dark DDoSer Malware for Sale

Figure 17. DDoS Attacks for Sale

The concern among law enforcement and intelligence agencies is the ability for criminals, terrorists, and spies to hide within the Deep Web. Their operations, communications, and plans can go undetected.

Furthermore, the use of advanced encryption, coupled with the Deep Web and Darknet, make it very difficult to identify and prosecute hackers and criminals even when their activities are known or revealed.

Chapter References

[1] (Bererns-Lee, 1989)

[2] (Tor, 2014)

[3] (Mansfield-Devine, 2009)

10

CONCLUSION

What started as a quest for knowledge and curiosity, has become a worldwide problem with no end in sight. The Center for Strategic and International Studies estimated the annual cost of cybercrime, hacking and information warfare at more than $445 billion annually [1].

Furthermore, the number and sophistication of attacks has steadily increased. In 2014, Target and Home Depot were victims of large scale point of sale attacks, and millions of credit and debit cards were stolen. Ebay lost the account information of over 233 million users, and Sony was attacked by North Korea in retaliation for the movie, "The Interview."

In June 2015 the federal government announced the Office of Personnel Management was hacked, and the personnel files of over 4 million federal employees. What is so concerning about this hack, the background investigation information for the employees was stolen. This includes the personal identifiable information of the employee, and their family members. As well as foreign contacts, foreign travel, and in some cases every detail of places employees have lived. A foreign intelligence agency could use this information for blackmail, extortion, and targeting of foreign relatives. The reporting points to China as the source of the attack [2].

As you can see, hacking, cybercrime, and information warfare are a serious issue, and it is only going to get worse. You can steps to protect yourself, but much of your information is in the hands of third parties, such as government agencies and retail outlets, and you have no control over how they protect your data.

I invite you to stay update on the latest hacking and cybercrime news at my website, www.hyslip.net and news on my books at www.bitwarsbook.com. Thank you for purchasing and reading my book. I hope you enjoyed it and learned a little along the way. For a non-technical review of each year's top hacks and attacks, check out BIT WARS: Hacking Report on Amazon.

Chapter References

[1] (Nakashima & Peterson, 2014)

[2] (Sternstein, 2015)

REFERENCES

Berners-Lee, T. (1989). Information Management: A Proposal. Retrieved from http://www.w3.org/History/1989/proposal.html

Mansfield-Devine, S. (2009). Darknets. *Computer Fraud & Security, 2009*(12), 4-6. Retrieved from http://dx.doi.org/10.1016/S1361-3723(09)70150-2

Tor. (2014). What is Tor?. Retrieved from https://www.torproject.org/docs/faq.html.en#WhatIsTor

Alhomoud, A., Awan, I., Disso, J., & Younas, M. (2013). A next-generation approach to combating botnets. *Computer, 46*(4), 62-66. Retrieved from http://doi.ieeecomputersociety.org/10.1109/MC.2013.67

Curtis, S. (2012, January 19). Barclays: 97 percent of data breaches still due to SQL injection. *Techworld*. Retrieved from http://news.techworld.com/security/3331283/barclays-97-percent-of-data-breaches-still-due-to-sql-injection/

Fachkha, C., Bou-Hard, E., & Debbabi, M. (2013, August). Towards a forecasting model for distributed denial of service activities. *Proceedings of the 2013 IEEE 12th International Symposium on Network Computing and Applications*, Cambridge, MA, 110-17. Retrieved from http://doi.ieeecomputersociety.org/10.1109/NCA.2013.13

OWASP. (2014). *Cross-site Scripting (XSS)*. Retrieved from https://www.owasp.org/index.php/Cross-site_Scripting_(XSS)

OWASP. (2014). *SQL Injection*. Retrieved from https://www.owasp.org/index.php/SQL_Injection.

Provos, N. (2012, June 19). Safe browsing – protecting web users for 5 years and counting. *Google Online Security Blog*. Retrieved from http://googleonlinesecurity.blogspot.jp/2012/06/safe-browsing-protecting-web-users-for.html

Roscini, M. (2014). *Cyber operations and the use of force in international law*. New York, NY: Oxford University Press

SANS & Mitre. (2011). *2011 CWE/SANS Top 25 Most Dangerous Software Errors*. Retrieved from http://cwe.mitre.org/top25/index.html

Ventre, D. (2013). Cyber Conflict: Competing National Perspectives. Indianapolis, IN: Wiley.

Arthur, C. (2013, May). LulzSec: What they did, who they were and how they were caught. *The Guardian*. Retrieved from http://www.theguardian.com/technology/2013/may/16/lulzsec-hacking-fbi-jail

Greenberg, A. (2012, January). Anonymous hackers hit DOJ, FBI, Universal Music, MPAA and RIAA after Megaupload takedown. *Forbes*. Retrieved from http://www.forbes.com/sites/andygreenberg/2012/01/19/anonymous-hackers-claims-attack-on-doj-universal-music-and-riaa-after-megaupload-takedown/

Hampson, N. (2012) Hacktivism: A new breed of protest in a networked world. *Boston College International Comparative Law Review, 35*(2). Retrieved from: http://lawdigitalcommons.bc.edu/iclr/vol35/iss2/6

Millis, E. (2011, July 19). FBI arrests 16 in anonymous hacking investigation.

CNET. Retrieved from http://www.cnet.com/news/fbi-arrests-16-in-anonymous-hacking-investigation/

Millis, E. (2012, March 12). Old-time hacktivists: Anonymous, you've crossed the line. *CNET*. Retrieved from http://www.cnet.com/news/old-time-hacktivists-anonymous-youve-crossed-the-line/

Paganini, P. (2013, October). Hacktivisim: Means and motiviations...what else? Infosec Institute. Retrieved from http://resources.infosecinstitute.com/hacktivism-means-and-motivations-what-else/

Simpson, I., & Roshan, M. (2013). U.S. soldier Manning gets 35 years for passing documents to wikileaks. Reuters. Retrieved from http://www.reuters.com/article/2013/08/21/us-usa-wikileaks-manning-idUSBRE97J0JI20130821

Alhomoud, A., Awan, I., Disso, J., & Younas, M. (2013). A next-generation approach to combating botnets. *Computer, 46*(4), 62-66. Retrieved from http://doi.ieeecomputersociety.org/10.1109/MC.2013.67

EC-Council. (2014). Certified Ethical Hacker. EC-Council. Retrieved from http://www.eccouncil.org/certification/certified-ethical-hacker

FBI. (2014). Common Fraud Schemes. Federal Bureau of Investigation. Retrieved from http://www.fbi.gov/scams-safety/fraud/fraud#419

FBI. (2014). GameOver Zeus Botnet Disrupted. Federal Bureau of Investigation. Retrieved from http://www.fbi.gov/news/stories/2014/june/gameover-zeus-botnet-disrupted

ISC2. (2014). Certified Information Systems Security Professional. ISC2. Retrieved from https://www.isc2.org/cissp/default.aspx

McAfee. (2014). Net Losses: Estimating the Global Cost of Cybercrime. Retrieved from http://www.mcafee.com/us/resources/reports/rp-economic-impact-cybercrime2.pdf

Taylor, R., Fritsch, E., and Liederback, J. (2014). Digital Crime and Digital Terrorism (3rd ed.). Sadle River, NJ: Prentice Hall.

Wallace, J., & Erickson, J. (1992). *Hard Drive, Bill Gates and the making of the Microsoft Empire*. Hoboken, NJ: Wiley Publishing.

Wang, T., & Yu, S. (2009). Centralized botnet detection by traffic aggregation. *Proceedings of the 2009 IEEE International Symposium on Parallel and Distributed Processing with Applications*, Chengdu, China, 86-93. Retrieved from http://dx.doi.org/10.1109/ISPA.2009.74

DOJ. (2014). U.S. Charges Five Chinese Military Hackers for Cyber Espionage Against U.S. Corporations and a Labor Organization for Commercial Advantage. [Press Release]. Department of Justice. Retrieved from http://www.justice.gov/opa/pr/us-charges-five-chinese-military-hackers-cyber-espionage-against-us-corporations-and-labor

Economist. (2014). The spy who hacked me. *The Economist*. Retrieved from http://www.economist.com/news/international/21635044-malicious-computer-code-making-spooks-job-easier-ever-spy-who-hacked-me

FBI. (2014). *Economic Espionage: Protecting American's Trade Secrets*. Retrieved from http://www.fbi.gov/about-us/investigate/counterintelligence/economic-espionage

Franceshi-Bicchierai, L. (2014). The 10 biggest revelations from Edward Snowden's leaks. Mashable.com. Retrieved from http://mashable.com/2014/06/05/edward-snowden-revelations/

Mandiant. (2013). *APT1: Exposing One of China's Cyber Espionage Units*. Mandiant. Retrieved from http://intelreport.mandiant.com/Mandiant_APT1_Report.pdf

NSA. (2014). Mission. [Web Site]. National Security Agency. Retrieved from https://www.nsa.gov/about/mission/index.shtml

Symantec. (2014). Regin: Top-tier espionage tool enables stealthy surveillance. Symantec. Retrieved from http://www.symantec.com/connect/blogs/regin-top-tier-espionage-tool-enables-stealthy-surveillance

Waldrop, M. (2008). *DARPA and the Internet revolution*. Defense Advanced Research Projects Agency. Retrieved from http://www.darpa.mil/WorkArea/DownloadAsset.aspx?id=2554

Hollis, D. (2008). Cyberwar case study: Georgia 2008. *Small Wars Journal*. Retrieved from http://smallwarsjournal.com/blog/journal/docs-temp/639-hollis.pdf

Kaspersky Lab. (2010). Kaspersky Lab provides its insights on Stuxnet worm.

Kaspersky Lab. Retrieved from
http://www.kaspersky.com/about/news/virus/2010/Kaspersky_Lab_provides_its
_insights_on_Stuxnet_worm

Kaspersky Lab. (2012). Kasperkey Lab experts provide in-depth analysis or
Flame's C&C infrastructure. *Kaspersky Lab*. Retrieved from
http://www.kaspersky.com/about/news/virus/2012/Kaspersky_Lab_Experts_Pro
vide_In_Depth_Analysis_of_Flames_Infrastructure

Matlack, C. (2014, March). Cyberwar in Ukraine falls short of Russia's full power.
Bloomberg Businesweek, Technology. Retrieved from
http://www.businessweek.com/articles/2014-03-10/cyberwar-in-ukraine-falls-far-
short-of-russias-full-powers

Rogers, M. (2014, March). Testimony before Senate Armed Services Committee.
U.S. Senate. Retrieved from http://www.armed-
services.senate.gov/download/hearing-03-11-14

United Nations Charter (1945). Chapter 1, Article 2, Section 4. Retrieved from
http://www.un.org/en/documents/charter/

United Nations Charter (1945). Chapter 7, Article 39, Article 42, and Article 51.
Retrieved from http://www.un.org/en/documents/charter/

Annual Country Reports on Terrorism, 22 U.S.C. § 2656f (2011).
Arimateia da Cruz, J. (2013, Nov). Terrorism, war, and cyber (In)security. *Small
Wars Journal*. Retrieved from http://smallwarsjournal.com/jrnl/art/terrorism-war-
and-cyber-insecurity

Denning, D. (2000). Cyberterrorism: The logic bomb versus the truck bomb. *Global Dialogue, 2*(4). Retrieved from http://www.worlddialogue.org/content.php?id=111

Easttom, C., & Taylor, J. (2011). *Computer Crime, Investigation, and the Law*. Boston, MA: Cengage Learning.

Federal Bureau of Investigation, 28 C.F.R. § 0.85. (2010).

Rollins, J., & Wilson, C. (2007). *Terrorist Capabilities for Cyberattack: Overview and Policy Issues*. Congressional Research Service, January 22, 2007. [Government Report]. Retrieved from www.dtic.mil/cgi-bin/GetTRDoc?AD=ADA463774

Singer, P., & Friedman, A. (2014). *Cybersecurity and Cyberwar What Everyone Needs to Know*. New York, NY: Oxford University Press

Theohary, C., & Rollins, J. (2011). *Terrorist Use of the Internet: Information Operations in Cyberspace*. Congressional Research Service, March 8, 2011 [Government Report]. Retrieved from http://fas.org/sgp/crs/terror/R41674.pdf

Weimann, G. (2006). Terror on the Internet: The New Arena, the New Challenges.
Washington, DC: United States Institute of Peace Press.

CERT-CC. (2014). About us. Retrieved from http://www.cert.org/about/

Chen, T., & Robert, J. (2004). The evolution of viruses and worms. In W. Chen (Ed.), *Statistical Methods of Computer Security*, (pp. 265-285). Boca Raton, FL: CRC Press.

Covert, C. (1983). High-tech hijinks seven curious teenagers wreak havox via computer. *Detroit Free Press*. Retrieved from http://timeline.textfiles.com/1983/

Leyden, J. (2012). The 30-year-old prank that became the first computer virus. *The Register*. Retrieved from http://www.theregister.co.uk/2012/12/14/first_virus_elk_cloner_creator_intervie wed/

McAfee. (2014). Net Losses: Estimating the Global Cost of Cybercrime. Retrieved from http://www.mcafee.com/us/resources/reports/rp-economic-impact-cybercrime2.pdf

Panetta, L. (2012, Oct). Remarks by Secretary Panetta on Cybersecurity to the Business Executives for National Security, New York, NY. [Press Release]. U.S. Department of Defense. Retrieved from http://www.defense.gov/transcripts/transcript.aspx?transcriptid=5136

Taylor, R., Fritsch, E., & Liederback, J. (2014). Digital Crime and Digital Terrorism (3rd ed.). Sadle River, NJ: Prentice Hall.

Wrinkler, I. (2007). *Zen and the Art of Information Security*. Waltham, MA: Elsevier.

Kim, R. & Lerman, D. (2015, Jan). U.S. Slaps New Sanctions on North Korea for Sony Hack and Vows Further Steps. Bloomberg. Retrieved from http://www.bloomberg.com/news/2015-01-02/u-s-slaps-new-sanctions-on-n-korea-in-response-to-sony-hack.html

Viswanatha , A. & Menn, J. (2015). In cyberattacks such as Sony strike, Obama turns to 'name and shame'. Reuters.com. Retrieved from http://www.reuters.com/article/2015/01/14/uk-usa-cybersecurity-idUSKBN0KN2E520150114

Joke, C. (2014). Interview transcript: former head of the NSA and commander of the US cyber command, General Keith Alexander. *Australian Financial Review*. Retrieved from http://www.afr.com/p/technology/interview_transcript_former_head_51yP0Cu1AQGUCs7WAC9ZVN

Zetter, K. (2011). Report: Stuxnet Hit 5 Gateway Targets on Its Way to Iranian Plant. *Wired*. Retrieved from http://www.wired.com/2011/02/stuxnet-five-main-target/

Rhoads, C. (2007). The twilight years of cap'n crunch. *The Wall Street Journal*. Retrieved from http://www.wsj.com/articles/SB116863379291775523

Christensen, J. (1999). The trials of Kevin Mitnick. CNN. Retrieved from http://www.cnn.com/SPECIALS/1999/mitnick.background/

Lawrence, D. & Riley, M. (2014). Home Depot Malware Hints at Different Hackers Than Target's. Business Week. Retrieved from http://www.businessweek.com/articles/2014-09-11/home-depot-hack-malware-points-to-different-hackers-than-targets

Smith, C. (2014). Expert who first revealed massive Target hack tells us how it happened. BGR. Retrieved from http://bgr.com/2014/01/16/how-was-target-hacked/

Mick, J. (2014). Appalling Negligence: Decade-Old Windows XPe Holes Led to Home Depot. Daily Tech. Retrieved from http://www.dailytech.com/Appalling+Negligence+DecadeOld+Windows+XPe+H oles+Led+to+Home+Depot+Hack/article36517.htm

Gillmor, D. (2014). As we sweat government surveillance, companies like Google collect our data. *The Guardian*. Retrieved from http://www.theguardian.com/commentisfree/2014/apr/ 18/corporations-google-should-not-sell-customer-data

Gokey, M. (2014). Apple, Facebook, Microsoft and Google break silence over government data collection. *Techtimes.com*. Retrieved from http://www.techtimes.com/articles/6427/20140503 /apple-facebook-microsoft-google-silence-government-data-collection.htm

Gumuchian, M., & Goldman, D. (2014). Security firm traces Target malware to Russia. *CNN*. Retrieved from http://www.cnn.com/2014/01/20/us/money-target-breach/

Shuster, S. (2010). The Russian hacker bust: Is the FBI only chasing mules? *Time*. Retrieved from http://content.time.com/time/world/article/0,8599,2023391,00.html

Risen, T. (2014). The New Mafia: Battling Hackers Like Organized Crime. US News and World Report. Retrieved from http://www.usnews.com/news/articles/2014/08/11/the-new-mafia-battling-hackers-like-organized-crime

McCaney, K. (2014). Nuclear arsenal finds security in 8-inch floppy disks. Defense Systems. Retrieved from http://defensesystems.com/articles/2014/04/29/af-8-inch-floppies-icbm-launch.aspx

Nakashima, E. & Peterson, A. (2014, June). Report: Cybercrime and espionage costs $445 billion annually. The Washington Post. Retrieved from http://www.washingtonpost.com/world/national-security/report-cybercrime-and-espionage-costs-445-billion-annually/2014/06/08/8995291c-ecce-11e3-9f5c-9075d5508f0a_story.html

Sternstein, A. (2015). OPM Breach Notificaiton Frustrates Hacked Feds. National Journal. Retrieved from http://www.nationaljournal.com/tech/opm-breach-notification-frustrates-hacked-feds-20150622

Other Works by Thomas Hyslip

Amazon #1 Hot New Release
BIT WARS: Hacking Report
Top Hacks and Attacks of 2014.

Amazon #1 Hot New Release
Proactive Botnet Detection: Through Characterization of Distributed Denial of Service Attacks

ABOUT THE AUTHOR

Dr. Thomas Hyslip is the Resident Agent in Charge of the Department of Defense, Defense Criminal Investigative Service (DCIS), Cyber Field Office, Eastern Resident Agency. Prior to joining the DCIS in 2007, Dr. Hyslip was a Special Agent with the US Environmental Protection Agency, Criminal Investigation Division, and the US Secret Service. Throughout his 17 years of federal law enforcement, Dr. Hyslip has specialized in cybercrime investigations and computer forensics. Dr. Hyslip has testified as an expert witness on computer forensics and network intrusions at numerous federal, state, and local courts.

Dr. Hyslip is also a Lieutenant Colonel in the U.S. Army Reserves and is currently assigned as an Assistant Professor of Preventive Medicine at the F. Edward Hébert School of Medicine, Uniformed Services University of the Health Sciences. LTC Hyslip has a mix of active duty and reserve assignments spanning over 20 years including assignments with the US African Command, Office of Inspector General, the Department of Defense, Office of Inspector General, and the US Army Reserve Information Operations Command. In 2005 LTC Hyslip deployed to Iraq with the 306th Military Police Battalion and earned a Bronze Star, Purple Heart, and Combat Action Badge.

Dr. Hyslip is currently an adjunct faculty member at Norwich University and Wake Technical Community College. Dr. Hyslip received his Doctor of Science degree in Information Assurance from Capitol College and his dissertation presented a new pro-active botnet detection technique. Dr. Hyslip previously obtained a Master of Science degree from East Carolina University and a Bachelor of Science degree from Clarkson University.

CPSIA information can be obtained
at www.ICGtesting.com
Printed in the USA
LVOW13s1812020117

519456LV00019B/1316/P

9 781514 673157